When We Wake
in the Night

When We Wake
in the Night

Poems by Tami Haaland

WordTech Editions

Published by WordTech Editions
P.O. Box 541106
Cincinnati, OH 45254-1106

ISBN: 9781936370740
LCCN: 2012939296

Poetry Editor: Kevin Walzer
Business Editor: Lori Jareo

Visit us on the web at www.wordtechweb.com

For my family

Acknowledgments

My thanks to the editors of the following publications in which earlier versions of these poems appeared.

5AM: "Mosaic," formerly titled "Intertextuality," "Liar," "After Dinner," "The Girl in the Monkey Cage," "My Red Velvet Self," "Rodin's Crouching Woman," "Given Time"; *Food For Us Blog:* "A Colander of Barley"; *High Desert Journal:* "When We Wake in the Night"; *Journal of Feminist Studies in Religion:* "Joyful Noise"; *Letters to the World:* "Reasons to Fly" *Mom Egg:* "Journey," formerly titled "Traveler"; *New Poets of the American West:* "Liar"; *Orison:* "After Dinner," "She Eats and Apple as the Salamander Observes," "Spelling"; *Pelucid Duck:* "Like Flowers in a Painting," "Soup," "Swim Lessons," "This Kitchen," "Bone"; *Platte Valley Review:* "Cherry Stone"; *Poems Across the Big Sky:* "Kathy Catches a Train"; *Rattapallax:* "Reasons to Fly"; *Red-Headed Step Child:* "Spring Burning in the Pasture," formerly titled "Burning Tree"; *South Dakota Review:* "These Roses," "October Snow," "Wild Goose"; *Stymie, A Journal of Sport and Literature:* "Pitch and Swing"; *Verse Daily:* "Mosaic," formerly titled "Intertextuality."

Many thanks to Sandra Alcosser, Malia Burgess, Dave Caserio, Cara Chamberlain, Jenny Factor, Sue Hart, Christene Holbert, Christopher Howell, Danell Jones, Bill Kamowski, Jim Peterson, Kathy Sabol and Virginia Tranell who read earlier versions of this work. Special thanks to Melissa Kwasny for her suggestions on revision and to Kevin Walzer, Lori Jareo, and WordTech for making this book possible. I am grateful to MSU Billings for sabbatical leave and faculty development funds that supported this work. My thanks to Dennis Kern, Jean Albus, and Christine

Holbert for their contributions to the cover design.

Notes

"After Dinner" refers to *Appalachian Journey*, a CD featuring Yo-Yo Ma and James Taylor. Line 7 is taken from Stephen Foster's "Hard Times Come Again No More" on this same CD. Other songs mentioned in this poem are "Mockingbird," a West Indies folk song, "Mack the Knife" by Kurt Weill with lyrics by Berthold Brecht, and "Summertime" from the opera *Porgy and Bess* by George Gershwin.

Contents

As Many Stories As Stars

Morning and Evening in Your Cup

Inquest

Late Constellations

Silvery World

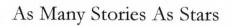

As Many Stories As Stars

Liar

He yells it before she slams the car door.
I'll walk home, she says to the closed window.

We finish her story in our own car.
In my version, she'll go to the corner,
he'll speed around the block, feel guilty,
return, and insist she get in.

In Irena's version he'll go where he's going.
She'll have to get there another way,
hitch hiking maybe or a long walk.

The ending is the same and we both know it,
the way we know there are only so many stories,
perfectly formed, and they enter us
each time in shadowy variation.

Or maybe there are as many stories
as stars and we don't see them until long
after they begin to shine, our recognition that dim.

It's summer. Our windows are down. This is
earlier in our lives and the wind whips our long hair.
We are the kind of women they joke about,
another kind of story, the blonds so dumb.

But we are smart enough to guess how this story
will end for the girl, smart enough to know
that if we keep on driving maybe

there's a better version up ahead just waiting
to pull its comb through our tangled hair.

The Kiss

My friend and I circle *The Kiss*, Rodin's
tribute to the lovers who were left, then caught
and killed for their failure to fail in
love. Look at the way they nearly resist
the embrace: their left arms not quite engaged,
her arm raised to encircle his shoulder and
his hand around but not resting, almost freed
from her hip. They sit close so ribs expanded
in breath must have let each body lean
to the other, and when breath began to coincide,
then each slipping to the space between
must have caused this kiss, my friend and I decide.
He stands on one side and I on the other.
Separate ends, a perfect diameter.

Exhibit

The woman in the butterfly pavilion
pretends she is a statue. Today's
docent says sex is in the air, so she stays,
hoping the shine and spark of cerulean
wings will settle, and thread-like feet will
attach to her arm. Though she can't detect
pheromones, the docent says they're like scent
to a fish in a slow-moving channel.
Behind closed doors the air is tropical:
philodendra grow to the greenhouse ceiling,
hibiscus and birds of paradise bloom.
A thousand wings seem so infallible.
The docent says these creatures are reeling.
They don't even eat once they leave the cocoon.

Budapest 1978

We sit at a table and smile
at the students. A tenor
in the corner delivers an aria,
high notes going higher
as he stands on his chair.
Then we sing a light number
from our repertoire,
then he sings, and we sing,
and he sings some more.

The one across the table
glances again. His girlfriend
doesn't like him smiling
at me. The students
want to give us mementos—
lapel pins they drop
in our hands—and he
chooses me. He gestures:
could he? My dress?

He slips his fingers under
the neckline, and the pin
moves in, his fingers
protecting my skin.
We look but don't
linger, and what words
could we speak? I remember
the place, the singing.
I still have the pin.

These Roses

I've been lazy this year, leaving old flowers
at the edge of the bed. Today I move
moldering leaves and stems to a bucket
and haul one load, then another
to the city compost bin. I don't trim
blooms until petals begin to fall,

though some say to collect them as soon
as buds open. When I work here, love songs,
their thorns and roses, fill my head
and music brings in the past. One day
my cousins call me to their sister-world.
I arrive on my bike, and the youngest

leads me to a chair, gives me ice. The oldest,
a college girl, holds a needle made
for heavy fabric. She has already pierced
her sisters' ears and it feels good to be
lined up, included, for the moment
not quite a sisterless girl. I shy from the cold

and when the needle stings, three voices
assure me it will be all right. One cousin
takes two cubes of ice in her hand and holds
my ear through pain of cold to numbness.
Then the needle enters and I can hear
the progress, its slow and sinewy course.

Kneeling near a ring of cement around
meandering and insistent brambles,
I dodge thorns and coax hard soil to soften
in water. Some plants, gone wild,
multiply vines and refuse to bloom. They
twine through everything and I let them.

Brambly Place

Who goes back and why? You say Eden,
I say silted waterways, overgrown blackberries,
bindweed, never mind the snakes. Go there
and eat the withered fruit, fine. It's not the same.
Brambly, too shady, no room for stars
through foliage. There are reasons you ate
and ran, reasons for someone to guard
the gate. Didn't the path lead away
for good reason? Thorns, yes, but take those away
and where are the roses, their mealy fruit?
No one said it would be easy.

Little Girl

She's with Grandma in front
of Grandma's house, backed
by a willow tree, gladiola and roses.

Who did she ever want
to please? But Grandma
seems half-pleased and annoyed.

No doubt Mother frowns
behind the lens, wants
to straighten this sassy face.

Maybe laughs, too.
Little girl with her mouth wide,
tongue out, yelling

at the camera. See her little
white purse full of treasure,
her white sandals?

She has things to do,
you can tell. Places to explore
beyond the frame,

and these women picking flowers
and taking pictures.
Why won't they let her go?

Given Time

Today the Sirens begin in the street,
the first dressed in plaid, her song
arriving before we see her slow step.
Then others, each with her part.
Their procession passes the house,
then again, inviting us to step outside.
Even I, mother of these boys,
want to sprint to the fence,
smile as they pass and think of
my own young voice and unlined face.

The boys watch as I make my move,
their ears sealed in headphones blasting
Guns and Roses, and they pull me back,
lash me to an elm in the back yard
with rope from the old baby swing.
What are they afraid of? Their mother might
join the Sirens, take up art songs, speak
in French? In Greek? The elm, sick in its center,
drips sap, but the leaves unfurl and
its finest branches tick-tick in the wind.

The Sirens have gone to the street
by the cliff. They may not return,
and I could be left under the full moon,
stars overhead. Overhead, cool air and
the massive sky. O Sirens, come back.
These men will not waste away, will not
listen enough to know your names.
But I am here, a lone woman bound

to this elm, and I would follow your voices.
In time, I could learn your song.

Spring Burning in the Pasture

Afterward she sees the brittle
ash tree, broken and ablaze.

She drags the hose, comes back
for a cane to make herself steady.

Inside and out. A little rest and
back to the task. No one to help.

It's midnight before she is
satisfied and goes to bed.

In the morning, there are flames,
the tree burning in its core.

And work: hoses and soaking.
Through the day licks of flame

come from the center. For days,
she can see it smolder.

To Cinderella on the Stair

Surprising how glass shoes carry you
past orchestra and sparkling gowns
down marble stairs. You lift your skirt
for speed, the fabric a sail in your wake.
The clock strikes. Your heart hesitates.

But look at the pearls, the white satin.
Must every woman wear this dress?
And in the shadows you see
the carriage, still a carriage,
ready to take you to the open road.

Consider whether to return to the hearth.
Think how long you might wait.

Morning and Evening
in Your Cup

The Husband Speaks

Tainted, is what she said
as she drank her tea. Coals
glowed scarlet in the night.
What I mean, she said, *is the way*
dust makes a layer in my cup.
The wind put it there, and I can taste

the flavor, the silica and scruff. Taste
dry air. She tossed a rock. *If I said—*
but she stopped, put her cup
by the fire. She stirred the coals
and watched one ember spiral into night.
Yesterday we agreed to come this way

though it was clear to me we were way
off course. Still I could taste
sweet creek smell and pine. By night-
fall, we had settled in. I said
it would be nice to watch until the coals
burned to nothing and we could fill a cup

of kindness . . . . She didn't like that, set her cup
upside down on a rock. Away
in the distance a coyote called. The coals
flickered, sank beneath soot, gave me a taste
of what was to come. I said
I didn't mean to forecast the night.

Embers multiply after midnight,
and I can't possibly sleep. At the creek I take a cup
of water and close my eyes. She said
this was it. I said I knew another way
off the mountain, easier, where we could taste
the last syllables of summer. I tend the coals

and listen for deer as she sleeps. The coals
seem to glow best when the night
engulfs and surrounds. So much darkness to taste
at once. Morning and evening in your cup.
It's good to be far away.
But now what have I said?

Bring the cup to your lips and taste,
I tell her. Once night is done, the coals are dust.
She looks away, hardly hears what I've said.

Stilled in Flight

Am I wrong to think we can divide time
and time again to get more of it?
Minutes slow on the clock. I've seen it happen
and am not fooled by the equal spaces
between numbers, the digital evolution
from one shining minute to the next.

I understand you will leave soon
and your decision, like every
passing minute, has its own mind.
The moon hoists itself into the sky,
the sun has gone down into sand.
A boy who likes baseball stays in his room,

makes low noises in the wake of every hit
he hears on the radio. This, too, takes time.
Meanwhile we wait: you in your far corner,
I in mine, and between us a prairie
of arid silence, so many
creatures gone to extinction.

Incessant winds bend buffalo grass,
crack soil, strip skin from bone.
Blackbirds press against the current,
stilled in flight. We make our passage
beside stone and lichen while minutes
race or stumble. Either way, they disappear.

Like Flowers in a Painting

It's October, early snow. We pull
geraniums inside where they will bloom
the winter, drip blossoms and leaves.

In the seventies, the East Germans
grew geraniums on their side
of the wall. The order?
Barbed wire, land mines, scarlet petals.

We were told not to take pictures
or even touch our bags. The guard
carried his machine gun through the bus
and confiscated nothing. There were

as many geraniums as land mines
placed evenly along the wall. Flowers
the color of these, tonight, in this room.

Soup

Green worm dying in a bowl on the counter.
Snow falling. Would it be kinder to put it
outside, let cold air take it or give it
a contained and warm place to spend its last?
The woman hovering near the sink
averts her eyes. Worms are too pliable, soft.

Once she found a snake dead two days
and did not hesitate to tear the flesh,
use sticks to pry rattles from bone.
Who can explain? She makes soup,
she sweeps, she washes her hands.
The children will be home soon and may
offer to take the worm. May eat the soup
and bread she has made, may tell her
stories of how their days have gone.

The counter is laden with poblanos,
broccoli and winter squash. Pumpkin
near the fire, zucchini and corn
in the center of the table. The garden
concluding in heaps. And the worm.
She could never touch the worm, only tip
the bowl and let it fall to the frosty ground.

Swim Lessons

Later, in bed, you will
remember the hard words,
the crunch of snow as wheels
pass into the middle lane,
the crescendo of anger at the light,
silence the rest of the way
to swim lessons.

Arguing over whether he will go—
he's going—whether he will go again.

He is eleven, big enough to know
what he wants, and you are forty,
not old enough to know
what to do. At the pool, his thin
new body slips into a world
that does not include you,
and you watch, holding his coat.

Pitch and Swing

Tonight we play the undefeated team, mostly
little guys. Base hitters and one slamaroo kid.
First inning one of our players hits a home run
and catches two flies. The whole team is hot,
then confused in the middle when a new pitcher
tricks the batters with his changeup.

The last few plays are slow motion. We're up
by one but a good hit can alter everything. I can't
help but think what it feels like on the other team,
to be twelve years old at bat, two out already, two
strikes and the next pitch coming in. Poor kid,
he'll feel like it was his fault. And then
he thwacks it, nice line drive to center field.
He smiles, and our team has to start over, more risk
because the kid on second could make it in.
Next kid, two strikes, and I feel sorry again.

Coach says that's the best thing about baseball.
You lose and you win. The batter digs his foot
into powder, ready to spring. The umpire and
catcher become concentric, the infield players
crouch toward the plate. It depends, now,
on the pitch. It depends on the swing, and now
the pitcher nods to the catcher, digs his toe in.

Spelling

How little the difference between *b* and *d*,
Each symmetrically opposed to the other. He
Sits at the table with his father.
The father reads words to him and he
Rights—no, *writes*—them down one word
Under the other, speaks them:
Get, at, about, ask, wrong, people,
Going, where. He spells them
Loudly, over and over. He knows these
Elements inside and out
(Sit, said), understands so many
Words beyond *like, begin, then* and *than.*
It's boring, for heaven's sake! To worry
These words into consistency, to waste
His life on *b* and *d, p* and *9.*
Since the teacher insists, however, since
Pupils must comply, he sets his mind
Each night to the recitation,
Leaning over his page, unsure how to spell
Little the same way each time.
In his mind's shadow place, letters
Needle each other when they meet, then
Gather stones to sink in a mossy lake.

Castle

The castle, there, on the living room floor
Holds knights who stare from the castle walls
Prepared for battle in the coming war.

They hold axes and swords; they bar the door
And climb the tower. One knight leans, then falls
From the castle to the living room floor.

The boy who built it doesn't keep score,
Though vile knights surround the castle walls.
Arrows will fly in the coming war.

He piles blocks high to reinforce the door.
A chopstick catapult hurls super balls
At the castle built on the living room floor.

If he had his way, hot oil would pour
From the top and scald down the walls.
The stakes are high in imaginary war.

A hundred knights here, but he would like more
To fill the castle and its banquet halls.
Through the long winter it will stay on the floor
And battles will rage in this specter of war.

Joyful Noise

When they are gone I miss them.
Nearly grown boys, the two of them
snapping towels in the kitchen,
throwing potatoes. *Someday I won't
stand between you*, I say as they lunge
in a mock fight. They tell me they
may lock me in another room
before then. Laughing, laughing.

They crash against each other
in the hall, the kitchen. *The pans
are hot*, I say. They hardly need me.
They set the table in a mad dance:
*I am the mashed potato man,
yes I am the mashed potato man.*
One of them skips with pan and masher,
the other bangs spoons on his head.

After Dinner

We play badminton with balloons
to Yo-Yo Ma's *Appalachian Journey.*
We don't keep score, just keep
balloons off the floor and move rackets
and bodies to the lyric phrase.
I sing with James Taylor,
let us pause in life's pleasures,
and I know this game may last a year,
off and on, or be gone tonight.

Summer nights, Dad tuned his guitar,
Ron played piano, and uncle came
with his mandolin. They knew
the same songs, "Mockingbird"
and "Mack the Knife," jammed
almost without speaking
until dawn. In the magic hour
before midnight, their voices
and melodies slipped into echoes

and I walked the dark hallway
to my room. If ancestors
watched in some quiet corner
to see how we kept ourselves
since they left, they could hear
"Summertime" in jazzy rhythms
and chords, remember keys
beneath fingers, fingers on strings,
a harmony of hands, the texture of night.

This Kitchen

This young man eats an open-faced sandwich and
explains multiple histories. I eat ravioli with sun-dried
tomatoes. Pages of this morning's paper, chaos on the
table. He says particles, we know, have many stories,
simultaneous timelines, but once they collect and turn
into organisms, these histories converge like waves in a
pool, *toddler in a puddle.* They cancel each other until we
have the single story, only this lunch, this discussion, *a
toy truck, a racing bike,* though really there were many
more—not theoretical, but real—crashing against each
other in a sandy-bottomed lake. We'll never know our
words or what's for dinner in that dissolving place. His
distilled account of what he has read fills an hour, and
we adjust ourselves against the glare and fading light
of this durable horizon.

Inquest

1. Penmanship

He chewed the end of his pencil,
sometimes bit the eraser almost off.
We'd tell him to stop and get to work.
He'd sit at the kitchen table, feet dangling,
copy in his penmanship book.

When we came in after the shop closed,
we could tell he'd been up to something.
He was old enough we didn't ask. Maybe
should have. And then the laughter,
the charm. He made us feel like he was

the best boy. Lucky then, but what could
we have done, and when? To have it back.

2. Now This

Who would have been ready?
Given five or ten more years,
how many would have prepared?

Except for those with foresight,
no one knows. You and I, for example,
are forever at the kitchen table

reading the paper, sipping coffee,
until the next thing happens,
and we look up in surprise.

3. The Nurse's Story

No one could have
gone into the cell.

I went with clothing,
with pills and water.

No one could have
opened the door.

Automatic.
Closed from below.

Who could have gone in, tied his
neck to a bar below the desk,

raised his feet to the bed
to keep his throat down?

No one could have
done this.

Who could hang a man
if he didn't want

to be hanged? No one
opened the door.

No one had a key.
No one tied the sheet.

4. Paperwork

It's all about getting you
into the filing cabinet.
Sure, we're sorry,

but kill yourself
and everything after that
is mop up: make sure

no one killed you, make sure
you did it yourself, make sure
you died as the coroner said.

5. A Day and Then Another

That's what we had and all
we hoped for. It was easier
if we didn't think *future*
or *years from now.*

Do you remember that time
at the creek, how he stood
in wind-blown apple blossoms?
It's what happiness ever amounts to.

6. Wind

Reminds you what you've
forgotten or never done.

Branches could topple,
tree roots give way.

Close the doors,
you hear ghosts.

Bills, calls, always
something coming.

Worse, what slips away.

7. The Verdict

It isn't what you think, but what
does that tell you? You nod your heads,
line up your notes with donuts and coffee.
You've seen the pictures, the autopsy
report. You know how capillaries
explode in the head when air and blood
can't circulate. A soft ligature, they said.

That's one truth. And the paperwork, another.
Syringes on the floor, efforts to revive,
automatic defibrillators assessing the chest.
You can hear it twenty times, but you can't see
what you need. They say in those last minutes
he wrote the alphabet, capital first, then lower case.
A steady hand. No one can say what it meant.

8. Fury

Better to be bitten
by a snake than this.
To fall from a mountain,
or have a cougar grab him
by the throat. More reason
in that. More sense.
Better a bear in spring,
a river over boulders,
better disease than this.

9. Said and Done

You know there were
questions beyond how
it occurred in that room.

The nagging sense you
could have seen
something.

And then everyone waiting,
the whole thing cut
and dried. They said take

your time, said this
is how to fill the forms.
Print neatly. Decide.

10. Moon and Stars

Here's how I think of it:
When he turned fourteen, we had that hard year—
he was gone two days before we saw
he'd been living in the hills south of the house,
coming down at night to eat from the old frig
we kept in the garage—that year,
when his birthday came, we were happy
despite his sullen looks and sad face.

I put out the best tablecloths.
We put a piñata in the maple out front,
shaped like the moon and filled with his favorite
chocolates. We bought a scooter like he'd wanted.
His dad took him fishing and I put everything
together, baked his favorite gold cake
and bought ice cream, called his friends
who arrived with cards and messy hair.
It was nearly dark. We put on music,
bought pizza, and he came home, then,
with cutthroat trout.

Now, in spite of the funeral,
the inquest, I think if I brighten
the tables, make some arrangement
to spill chocolate from moons and stars
suspended in maple, invite everyone
he ever loved, I think he might know
he is welcome. No, more than that.
He is someone we are tied to.

11. In Secret I Make My Plea

I look at his picture.
Don't die, I say. The face
looks back. *Don't.*

Late Constellations

When We Wake in the Night

Those of you who sleep through
don't know what you're missing:
late constellations, owls in tamarack,
shadows on carpet, cool floors.

We know who leaves lights on.
We know when the morning paper
arrives, how the carrier idles her car,
parks, walks three houses, and goes.

In the dark, the leaden feeling
of children growing away pulls
for attention. The son who didn't get
his swing set no longer needs one.

If we sit on the porch in summer
or fall, maybe we hear a grey catbird,
its single descending call over water.
It likes sumac, yellow dock, the dark.

Mosaic

You bring your sadness
to someone else's story
then miss a key point,

dwelling, as you are, on memories,
the grave goods you buried
and meant to forget.

Then you find a shovel
and begin digging
only to lose the plot

except where it corresponds
to your own story, proof
that your life is predestined,

a patterned course. You thought
you had changed, become a better
listener, but the story is over

and you can't remember
the ending. Those fragments
you've unearthed

still catch the light.
If only they were whole again
and belonged to you.

How Geometry Came into Play

It was a day that began
at the end of a rope
and promised wilder frays.

Our subject walked
through an empty parking lot,
eyes on asphalt gray.

A magpie stepped
around a corner; then
bird and person circled

an invisible center.
Their respective steps
beneath a skiff of pine

lightened the way.
Two ends of a string
tightened and turned

by who knows what
that September day.

Traveler

You are riding in the back as always.
The fog comes up and the road is icy.

The sun goes down. You catch
glimpses of the center line, a white-rimmed edge.

And now the downhill part, curving
with patches of gravel.

Of course there is a destination
and there will be towns along the way.

The dog wakes and your children scrape ice
from their windows. Somewhere above,

you see through angular crystals
how the nearly full moon dispenses light,

and you come to a shallow valley,
snow-covered sage brush, fields

where you know pheasant and turkey feed
in the daylight. But this is late,

the day creatures are asleep,
and your family continues in the dark.

Kid Stuff

Stella told the story about hitting
her young brother mid-back
until he crumpled and cried
on the carpet and Stella became
sorry, sorry she had hit so hard,
then ran and locked herself
in the bathroom while he fumed
red-faced outside the door.
It had been the last time
or one of the last times they fought.
They were home, no parents anywhere.
She felt she had done real damage
watching pain explode from another.

Can't Help

Can't help but consider those last moments,
a decision to go forward, then she sees
she won't make it to shore. The look on her face.

It's the work of the dark night, reaching
into those other lives, what it seems
they might be or have been. Making a story

of their leaving, their altered shapes.
And then reaching, unraveling,
sending it backward from darkness:

Swim harder. Think first. I wish you could fly.
Pause here. Say more. Put the gun down.

Catalog Shopping

In recent years her eyes moved
away from clothes to dwell on models,

examined lines in their smiles and cheeks,
wondered about hair color, the bra's lift.

The old wants surfaced: if her legs
had been longer, hair darker, skin olive—

or hair lighter, skin ivory, eyes blue.
And the new: were her lips full as these?

Did her hair catch the light? After all these years
should she begin to wear heels?

The knuckles, the hands, those lines at the wrist,
the skin below the chin when the neck twists.

If she continued the study, perhaps
she could sketch the body's passage in words,

begin to fathom how surface and fold
explain the enigma of skin.

Triangles

In
geometry,
triangles were
my favorite shape, the
formulas for their volume or
parameters more fun to remember
and use, though, as a shape less practical
than lines, which have somewhere to go, or
quadrilaterals, especially squares or rectangles which
say *fill me, I will contain*. But triangles with their cramped
corners and broad centers never seemed to beg for filling nor
head out on their own, yet if you make them three-dimensional, by
giving four of them a square base, you have a mystery, an elaborate tomb.

Bone

Set bone and uncast it in eight weeks.
Muscles heal slow, hold their hurts, their habits,
and make bone go. Pull bone to the piano,
let eye train muscle, see bone reach.

Bone stays. Bone shines. Bone can sit on a desk
and never move. Bone can hide in sand
until children dig. Look! Here comes bone.

Skull of a deer on a coulee bank. Bone, like rock.
Bone, like hammer. You can count bones, count
on bone. No quick dissolve. No slippery rot.
What we come down to is bone.

Brief Meditation

Who needs memento mori
when the people around you are dying?
Of course you see how the story

applies to you. No use lying
about your own demise,
breath and silence vying

for a host: so sad, so wise.
You stand and wait
and the line is moving. Your cries

against fate and careless night
follow one more into her dying.
Next day you sit and stare at your plate,

wondering about your place in line,
wondering if you've been left behind.

Your Emergency Waits

If you haven't met it, you will.
It sits somewhere on a sofa watching reruns
until the time is right.

It will come to your door
and cross your threshold unannounced.
No matter how you think it will look,

how you may have planned,
it will find ways to surprise you.
This is the advantage of time:

Hasn't it waited for this moment?
Didn't it always foresee this collision?
You will gasp, maybe cry or shriek.

Your emergency has offered you
this gift. It will lean into you. It will become
a familiar weight against your shoulder.

Sooner or later you will put your arm
around it. You will learn the pattern
of its breath, how it occurs, despite your panic,

in a steady and predictable way. It will look
in your refrigerator; shuffle your papers.
Your emergency will learn your floor plan,

and in time it will call you home.
It will become so ordinary,
it will be invisible to strangers, as subtle

as the scar where a pine splinter
from the playground drove into your shin.
At the time it seemed like terrible damage.

Conversations

For years, she has tried
to convince her newly dead
relatives and friends either
to return or be on their way.
Who can say why this happens—
mostly in dream—or why
she feels compelled to carry on
the conversations. Some sit
and stare. She can see
they aren't happy. Some speak,
or they listen. They hover
or perform, demonstrate a task,
throw her a prayer book, teach her
to sing, cook, escape.

They aren't scary like the first ones
when she was a girl, the ones
who came in bloodied from war.
Some are gracious. A teacher,
for example, buys coffee
and gives her sugared berries.
None of them will consider
returning, and she can see how—
after they recover from
their demise—there is plenty
to worry about without
a body, plenty to do
and say, visits to make.
As always, rooms to prepare.

Rodin's *Crouching Woman*

You don't know
the weight,
how calves ache,
back, neck, worse
the underbelly
scarred. Not what
anyone can see.

If I look up,
light slaps the eyes.
The head wants
what is still, cool,
the shadow.
Make me small,
O Lord,
invisible.

Yammer

What are you doing, you gulls, you sparrows,
and why do you hover over this snowy road?

Maybe you planned to be farther south.
Out of habit, you're after insects that aren't there.

I'm conversing with people who aren't here—
and I could tell you what they'd say.

If it weren't so late, I might join you in the air,
see what it's like to navigate a gray sky.

Instead I'm concentrating on this icy road, cars ahead
and behind, careful not to brake so hard I fishtail and slide.

Too many people are dying down here. Does that happen
to you too? One day your friends are with you

and then they disappear? I don't like winter much or a sink
full of dishes, the dog restless and pacing in the kitchen,

though I'm happy as anyone to make castles from sand.
And why do you spend so much time inland?

Why wait for mice the plow turns up?
Wouldn't you rather catch starfish in the tide

still writhing as they fall from their underwater sky?
You're in the wrong place, gulls, and so am I.

Silvery World

October Snow

As you have taught, I size up the sky,
pay less attention to wet-fallen leaves
than the angle of light through a filter
of clouds. At home, I cut October's
iced rose buds, still destined to unfurl,
the evidence there in the sheltered petals.
Next, Swiss chard kept from tonight's
hard freeze: yellow and red stems, waxy leaves
spread on the counter before dinner.
And now, the painter in you would look
to the canvas, late afternoon drama,
storm clouds and shadow roiling.
You would observe how light
descends on mountain ash, the berries
heavy in the intimacy of snow,
and watch cedar wax wings cluster
to shake the tree from its still life.

Color and Song

To the one who sets up the canvas:
sky in broad strokes,
the brush large, then clouds,
background before pine needles, the lake
before a tanager on the near shore.

To the one who replaces the E-string
and tunes guitar to piano,
guides fingers to keyboard, fingers to frets,
demands runs and scales and thinks it best
to begin this one on middle C.

To the one who adds movement,
which is time, to the canvas,
and to time for blending notes
and brush strokes, turpentine and guitar pick,
E-string and boar bristle.

For burnt sienna and celandine, ochre
and azure, the knife, the circular arrangement
of pigment on palette.
For *do, mi* and *sol,* the odor of oils,
a ready canvas, for color and song.

Fish Creek Bridge

Twenty years, and I still feel railroad ties
beneath my feet, space between showing us
a three hundred foot drop to the creek.
We step beside rails, but if a train comes
we plan our exit to a wooden platform
with nothing to prevent us from falling off.
Swallows glide and dive, the caddis flies swarm
along the upper creek as we step down
onto sand. Then, in the half darkness past sunset
we retrace our light and cautious steps
across splintered pine, the dizzy falling
of imagination, each glance calling
out the details: one body caught in sight
of the other body that stays or leaps.

Stranger Refutes the Dreamer

Blue Jay flies to its tree
from the corner of the church. Complains,
of course. Outside a window at dawn,
it squawks the world awake.

No, I don't know what kind
of tree, don't know why the jay
does what it does. What makes
him think we want to listen?

We carry on in space, live out
our time, can only do
so much, only know so much.
No reason to care about blue jays.

Which is why you need to
come in from this sunshine,
come in where walls
surround you and the sun

can only hit you through glass.
Make it stained glass and you get
half the worrisome rays, a defined
and limited space.

You know where you are then,
and that is as much as you need
to know. But I see how you
deceive yourself about more.

Pay attention: if you want to stare
at treetops and picture yourself
in flight, you take your chances.
You can't hope to know all the names.

Cherry Stone

A small room fills with music,
rolling hills of sung melody. I eat toast
and jam, drink tea. Life, it appears,
is simple, and I simply live
at my desk, waiting for the next
good book, the next song, the next.

Why, then, do I want to drive my car
into the western sun, defy gravity,
breathe underwater, know the rhythm
of gills? Why, when I find a seed
in my jam, must I summon the dark earth
that engendered the tree, the roots
navigating a thousand years of humus
to produce this moment's fruit?

Reasons to Fly

If Icarus were forty, he could balance
his course between sea and sun.

You see the bowl of flicker feathers,
the glorious underside of a cardinal,

and once you get over your fear
of heights, what could stop you?

You'll understand things that traverse the sky,
the meandering gnat, the hawk's claws.

Why not practice now, before spirit separates
from body, observing its static serenity?

You could see past sadness,
find the tangible interior of clouds.

Consider the cold fire of stars at your back,
the ground's contours and currents below.

It's what every restless ounce of you has
always wanted, the inscrutable air.

Crossing the Marias

One of us held barbed wires
and the rest stepped through
to scramble after a leader,
or abandon leaders for
another way, stopping
for stones, skirting cactus
and gullies to the river.

Who proposed the crossing?
Shoes off, or on?
Feet into current, knees,
hips. Wavering on moss.
We laughed, of course.
Couldn't swim, and
there was no help for falling.

Water held us in leg locks,
our force against it,
toes inching along
the stony bottom.
Then water receded.
We ascended: hips, knees,
calves, and feet.

Whatever we hoped for,
we found no newness
but lingered, wanting surprise.
It was late summer.
Carp lurked beneath
undercut banks. Sun
sparked the current along.

The Girl in the Monkey Cage

The monkey pulled at her ear, peeked
into her sleeve, sorted through hair and
nibbled at imaginary lice. It let her go then

and lay down for her. She grazed fingers
over ribs, parted strands down to pale skin,
and when it turned, she walked her hands

from skull over lean body to bony tail.
The monkey sat up and yanked her hair, her
whole head down, brushed fingers into

her blouse, along her spine, and bit
her golden chain. I wanted to be the girl
in the monkey cage, to know how her mind

shifts when those fingers slip over skin.
To know teeth like watery pearls on the scalp,
mist of its breath on lashes and lobes.

My Red Velvet Self

All day my red velvet self
has been waiting to go outside.

It's hard to say what I will do
having escaped a dark life in the closet.

My long sleeves, my buckle back
and button front can't wait

to step out from fleece and pile,
the heavy canvas of winter.

Dance? Could be I will twirl
and make a scene, cut up the ballroom

or preen on the street. I'll never
be mistaken for my beige,

my gabardine self, left home
to blend with kitchen tile.

Watch me run the stairs.
See how I leave a room?

My red velvet bravery,
these daring feet.

She Eats an Apple
as the Salamander Observes

It swims in a stainless steel bowl
where I might wash spinach on another day.
A flat rock placed strategically makes it feel
safe, the way people in the Titanic felt safe
when they experienced the merest shudder
and went on dancing or climbing into bed.

Salamanders don't eat apples that I know of,
preferring insects or earthworms, but this one
seems mildly interested as I bite—
black dot of pupil in a gold ring meeting
the rods and pupil of my own brown eye.
It has four fingers on the front, five
on the back, its skin slick and spotted, its face
unlined. We share mostly the same DNA,
mapped like cities and farms on a curving road.

Sometimes it looks like a dog, jumping up
to pull crickets from our fingers. Sometimes
it's like a baby, round eyes spread wide
on its skull. It dives when I slice beans and
boil pasta. I don't think *dirty salamander*
on the counter. I don't think *in my way.*
I think *don't splash, don't startle,*
don't disturb this silvery world.

A Colander of Barley

The smell, once water has rinsed it,
is like a field of ripe grain, or the grain held
in a truck, and if you climb the steel side,
one foot lodged on the hubcap, the other
on the wheel, and pull your body upward,
your hands holding to tarp hooks, and lift toes
onto the rim of the truck box, rest your ribs
against the side, you will see beetles
and grasshoppers among the hulled kernels.
Water stirs and resurrects harvest dust:
sun beating on abundance, the moist heat
of grain collected in steel, hands
plunging and lifting, the grain spilling back.

Kathy Catches a Train

I am stuck on twenty-seventh street behind three cars
in the turn lane. I am late to meet my friend who walks north
while I drive south so we can stop midway at McCormick Café.

Then the trains come, freighters hauling coal and boards. One train
blocks twenty-seventh and the crossing arms come down.
My light is red, and too much traffic has backed up.

Waiting and waiting. But then, here comes Kathy.
She's been stuck behind that train too, and, impatient now,
she strides past the fallen arms and climbs the engine's stairs.

She wears her brown plaid jacket, and I can see she plans to step down
the stairs to this side of the tracks, but the train starts to move.
She holds the rail, and afraid to risk falling beneath wheels,

she stays, surprised and still. In a minute, she's behind a brick building
heading west. I wonder if she'll let go of the rail and go inside
or if she'll hang on until they find her and pry her loose. I wonder

when the people at work will realize she hasn't come back from lunch,
and when her husband will find out she hasn't stayed late at the office.
Surely the engineer will offer shelter as they climb the continental divide.

There will be food. I bet they stop sometimes, and she could
get off wherever she likes. Of course I'll hear from her. She'll call
and tell me about the island she inhabits or her winter vacation

in Brazil. I'll tell her how she looked that day, boldly impatient
when her road was blocked, the machine taking her from her settled life.

No Hands

Pack on her back, hair in a ponytail.
I see her after she passes but hear
her rubber-on-asphalt arrival
and departure as if I am standing near
railroad tracks, only I am a morning
walker, and she, a no-hands rider
steering her bike down a curving street.
Sun out, it could be any summer.

And now I am ten, a no-hands girl with hair
caught in wind. This is a dirt road, a prairie,
a world of blue above. The girl becomes
me, then it's she and I, then she. Time loves
this trick, knows I will trip in a moment, skip
into memory, body sailing, hands free.

Wild Goose

Solitary,
the wild goose follows a river,
speaking its own tongue.

> Dawn, she alone wakes
> among her companions.

It flies west. An hour
from now, sun will illumine
east-flowing currents.

> She is a girl, awake
> on sandstone, or used to be.

The goose call does what
moving sounds do: grows louder,
then smaller, then goes.

> She should, she should. For a long
> time now, her life parceled out.

In dim light, the chill
of summer morning. Again
she hears the current.

ल ल ल ल ल ल

Made in the USA
Las Vegas, NV
25 July 2024

92907908R00062